In a Flash of Lightning

Fifty-four Poems of Cosmic Vision

IN A FLASH OF LIGHTNING

FIFTY-FOUR POEMS
OF COSMIC VISION

ZHAO SI

TRANSLATED BY

Bruce Meyer

with

Xuan Yuan and Tim Lilburn

EXILE
editions

singular fiction, poetry, nonfiction, translation, drama, and graphic books

Library and Archives Canada Cataloguing in Publication

Title: In a flash of lightning : fifty-four poems of cosmic vision / Zhao Si ; translated
by Bruce Meyer with Xuan Yuan and Tim Lilburn.
Other titles: Poems. Selections. English.
Names: Si, Zhao, 1972- author. | Meyer, Bruce, 1957- translator. | Xuan, Yuan,
translator. | Lilburn, Tim, 1950- translator.
Description: Translated from the Chinese; poems originally published in Bai wu ya and
Xiao shi, ji yi.
Identifiers: Canadiana (print) 20210271914 | Canadiana (ebook) 20210277831 |
ISBN 9781550969412 (softcover) | ISBN 9781550969429 (EPUB) |
ISBN 9781550969436 (Kindle) | ISBN 9781550969443 (PDF)
Classification: LCC PL2960.I2 A2 2021 | DDC 895.11/6—dc23

Published by Exile Editions Ltd ~ www.ExileEditions.com
144483 Southgate Road 14, Holstein, Ontario, N0G 2A0

We gratefully acknowledge the Government of Canada and Ontario Creates for
their financial support toward our publishing activities.

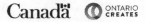

Canadian sales representation: The Canadian Manda Group, 664 Annette Street,
Toronto ON M6S 2C8 www.mandagroup.com 416 516 0911

North American and international distribution, and U.S. sales:
Independent Publishers Group, 814 North Franklin Street,
Chicago IL 60610 www.ipgbook.com toll free: 1 800 888 4741

MIX
Paper
FSC® C100212
www.fsc.org

For my parents, sister
and
eternal kinship through poetry

INTRODUCTION
by Bruce Meyer

As is the case with much contemporary Chinese poetry, the work of Zhao Si has been unknown in Canada until now. Crossing linguistic, cultural, and geographic distances is difficult, yet in the case of Zhao Si we have a poet who demonstrates a profound awareness not only of her own traditions and mythology but of the literature and legends that inform Western poetry. Her work is a weft of allusions, references, and traditions, and she creates a poetry of science as easily and as deftly as she handles her understanding of Homer and Polish poetry. What is presented here, for the first time in Canada, is a volume of poetry that astounds in its breadth and international scope.

Zhao Si is a poet of the infinite. She perceives enormous questions – the structure of the universe, the way in which time expands and contracts, and the realms of quantum physics and Hawking radiations – in the same breath as she watches a beggar outside a subway station, a woman riding a bicycle through rain, or a homeless man with skin maladies. Her poems demonstrate a meeting of science, actuality, and the unconscious that ranges from the specific, the world around her, to the invisible, a world that can only be described in the broad abstract terms of physics and mathematics. In a breathtaking diversity of scope and language, she sees everything with an omniscient vision that is truly startling, and reminds her readers (without directly saying so) of Elizabeth Bishop's dictum that a poem is a million things happening at once. A keen observer of what exists right before her eyes, Zhao Si is constantly reminding her reader that the macrocosm exists in the microcosm, that what is visible in the finite is also to be perceived in the infinite if we are willing to open our eyes.

The whirlpools and eddies that we encounter in the opening poems of this collection expand, through the powers of her expansive vision, into the theoretical structure of the universe. What can terrify us when beheld on a cosmic scale are the same structures that in their small, human expressions, are gentle, obvious, and yet so easily overlooked when we take the time to notice them in the familiarities of daily life. As such, Zhao Si is a poet of scale, and her ability to equate the vastness of time and space with the small things of life – a bird market, lovers' promise padlocks on a German bridge, or a simple walk along a beach at sunrise – are challenging to many readers, and especially to her translators. Zhao Si's sense of the infinite as she expresses it in her Chinese poetry is a test of the specificity and the concreteness of the English language.

I am reminded of conversations I had with British poets and translators, Christopher Middleton and Charles Tomlinson. Middleton's great test of his translation skills was the poetry of Rainer Maria Rilke, in particular "The Duino Elegies," where the complexities of the soul and the vastness of means at Rilke's disposal to engage the soul through poetry point away from the specific. In *Poetry and Metamorphosis,* a book that every English translator should read, Charles Tomlinson finds a solution to the issue of difficulty faced by those who seek to take poems from other languages and make them into English language poetry. The solution, Tomlinson notes, is to enable the poems to live new lives in English, bend to the laws of a language that insists on pointing to things rather than dwelling in abstracts. Chinese poetry, a tradition that is centuries older than the English tradition and that possesses the means of expressing breadth and idea without ever coming down to earth, is a difficult matter when it comes to doing justice to its beautiful abstractions.

What makes this volume of poetry different from other books of Chinese poetry I have read and wrestled with is the fact the Zhao Si is a poet who, either through her predilection for an international vision, or through her strong background in European verse, spans the gap between the Eastern mind and the Western. And it is this ability to bridge traditions, to ask her readers to see the infinite in the finite, that makes this volume an important dialogue that brings Chinese and English readers together.

Apostle

I am made of stories
that are woven to become a legend
words in a diaspora
tied to the feet of each poem.

Children

They disappeared swiftly
without a trace. Coiling waves, whirled-away time,
each a spinning vortex, soft curling locks of hair,
bright smiles.

Acres and acres vanished before
they were dim reflections of stars on the Earth.
Cherubim who borrow the first appearance of the soul,
the quantum fluctuations of their iridescent wings;
stars, too distant from the Earth,
reflections wavering.

Coils and coils, whirled away time, soft angels,
reflections of stars vanished in a blink.

Sighs

for all the slaughtered victims

I hear, I hear the flock of rain, crowing, rushing out of stirred crowds,
a deluge of chaos and fright, laughing, roars of laughter
crashing into the Wailing Wall. Triumphant karma holds a sharp blade
in its mouth and slices the sigh into pieces; one piece, two pieces,
feathers flutter, dancing. You emerge among the whirling sleet.
What is beyond mortal imagination arises –
the appointed time has come –
the sky shatters into snowflakes.
I see, I see the suffering, the *dukha* of your heart, as it swells up, up
until an angel thunders out; he flexes the roots
of his dark, unfamiliar wings, pressing against the cyclone
from an emptiness in the heart, then bows his head to peck
an immense, petrified world with his sharp beak. Already stone,
you, an enormous sigh, stand upright but burn inside.
A fire wall, a wall of fire burns darkly and damply, smoking
palely and bitterly, collapses, buries, buries the eternal sighs.

Riding

My outcast soul opens to you like a jellyfish,
transparent, innocent, blithe to your tentacles' sting.
Only in your gaze – it feels warm and intimate.
You love it pathetically, don't you?
It is destined to belong to you;
infiltrating you, instantly a dazzling water-green
rocking to the motion of a subway, a huge kettle –
and I am a drop that rides in you.
With one glance, you know me.
Inside me, water molecules mimic your rocking, don't they?
Suck it!
Too noisy this isolation.
I sere and wither in your name
and then become a ball of bright silver
     a promise to give you
     a satellite in your orbit
     rising from your palms.

Love Dance

Those weary faces are my face, too;
those hopeless hearts, all my heart;
those struggling people struggle inside me;
this tattered world is the clothing I also have to wear;
but earthly happiness fails to satisfy my desiring soul.
Yet, in each illuminating flash of divine creation,
I see that tacit, esoteric congenital hold
that unfolds its illustrious phoenix tail,
buttressing my waist with empathy
in the brutal dance to survive.

Sacrificial Meat

A pair of crumpled, muddy jeans
lie weirdly on the street after the rain
looking like a weather-beaten face.
Are they the aftermath of violence
or simply abandoned clothing?

People with weary faces wait for the bus,
swarm at the station to be on time.
When the bus comes, the crowd stirs
as if a flock of raptors dashing toward
sacrificial meat.

This morning, strangely,
my impaired vision sees
the darkest part of fate that keeps apace
with the scapegoat tied to its doom.

Translating

You are the thunder of God,
I, the echo of you.
You are the fullness of Him.
I am the seven thousand signs recorded
over seven centuries by the Babylonians.
The signs persist with anecdotal bliss.
They make you believe in your starry foresight
after you are dispossessed
of the divine strength and the vision you abandoned.
I am not alone; with me
dolphins are singing about my milk-white soul
inhabited from generation to generation.
A dying star lives in a spurious heart;
Lord Odin is old. Evil is everlasting.
The only new things are being forgotten;
shoals of deep-sea fish with big mouths, big eyes,
glowing in their bioluminescence.
You widen my horizon.
I am your seed, yet I make my own life.
You are the ancient tragedy spanning Bifröst;
I am the modern strategy of deriving The Theory.
You are the instrument through which
God transforms you to be His purpose.
I am the huge hammer
circling to crack God's head.
You are an ancient deity.
I am modern science.

Emptying

In an autumn gust, a small car
chugging hard, leaves chug along
to the rhythm of exodus & return. A row of green turtles
roll onto their yellow bellies and float down the street;
wearing a fox mask, perching on a tree,
sitting on a riverbank, autumn howls and watches;
stars inside the traffic lights quit work early
on Thanksgiving afternoon; waves of cars
chugging and stalling. The fox hangs its sighs
on leaves fly back to home, waves of crunchy bitterness in the mouth,
the taste of west wind, the arrival of bitterness unleashes
the hand of autumn gusts; a splendour hereto unseen,
a grand occasion, the aphasic master of the resplendent turnabout,
clears his throat, raises his song in the empty warehouse of autumn.

A Dot

Running a race against destruction, nowhere to hide: a dot runs;
destruction blossoms in ellipsis, large dust-flakes rain down;
a dot runs, desperately, heart full from passing through scudded clouds
across the sky, across the fallen homeland, piercing the core of evil
      beyond imagination.
An angel looks back; nowhere to shelter; who is demolishing, demolishing
everything with such speed? Homeless, helpless, I run and run and run
      at a loss, nowhere to stop,
a dot running on tips of needles, on blades of knives and chopping boards,
a dot, tiny as a conjured mote – all that remains of my soul,
a dot cast by an urgency to survive. Thank God!
I ride and ride and ride a flower parachute, three flower umbrellas,
against waves of spraying dangers, incessant crises that swell, swell, swell…
One must do something! One dot kicks a shot and the bullets fly;
another dot dashes out like a slant shot from a barrel,
another, riding on bees, jumbo mount buzzing about, at least nine dots
break through the nine millimeter pellet lights in the hell-deep towering
of terror. A twinkle of dots fall,
hopes splash in a star burst!
Struggle! Struggle! Take two sewing needles in my hand,
threefold be the curse I weave and weave and weave around disorder's head,
a bundle of self-preservation, a preaching finger
covers me; I lie down beneath the sky heading against the morning sun and it
      flames out.

Home

for master, especially Bruno Schultz

You are something I've never seen before but love innately,
out of a drifting black forest, a town of bursting light
warm, dazzling, beyond any limits.
A thread of passion
runs through me, suspended behind
a huge cobwebbed soul, shining with inexpressible connections
woven by each street built on a need to belong
in the night breezes of April, a three-sided blade
of smells, listening
to lofty phantoms, a déjà vu of foreign kinsfolk
who, for generations, lived in these streets;
they rise up one after another
until high above they are, like high-noon suns,
cast heavy thought-shadows on a place with nowhere to hide.

Silver

Praying for nothing except not to be toppled, nothing except not to fall,
nothing except a reed to be raised up when it is bruised,
a smoldering wick that will not be extinguished.
Before the age-old curtain of irksome noise is drawn,
a person gradually becomes intimate with a music
of the slow threading voice of raindrops.
Each and every glint of raining lines on sad metal strings
breaks into pieces, spatters still
tears of no return; they are
in the mosaic of voice of wheels, pedestrians, traffic signals,
huge flashing screens, steely concrete buildings, city light
modeled on a symphony and draw randomly in a silver world
on the glass walls of each and every skyscraper.

Addicted

The hunter has hooked limbs,
and the captured can never shake them off;
with each passing day, the hunter becomes
sharpened by it,
burned by its fire,
wrapped by its shroud,
staggering and stumbling all the way,
puffed out, blown away,
made a fool, cleaved asunder,
enlightened by the miraculous brightness of the gloaming,
thrown away and retrieved by the hunt itself,
kicked, until he eventually faces the hunted.

Suddenly, the hunt collapses.
A dowsing rod in-hand, the hunter taps the corpse
and wonders who granted him such power?

But then, wretched and battered, the hunter suffers,
beholding the criss-crossed scars marked on his limb's memory,
stretching and morphing into a map of many roads
while another hunter, hesitantly, is sprouting his beaked head.

In a Flash of Lightning

All day, I've dipped into the fantastic moment,
sunshine dismissed, all things clean and crystal,
leaves like green feathers, sunlight, clouds of white roses
blooming one after another.
I've walked on the street as if walking on the bow of the world's ship,
the tranquility spreading in the parting of the rippling wind,
reflected in the azure infinity lake of my heart.
Yet an unknown sound arises, terse,
out of a giant mirrored face – its withy outline opens,
purity settles in its shiny and silvery depth.
Myriads of changes evaded, reserved and restrained,
fold in on themselves
before suddenly vanishing.
In the silence of waiting, a pearl-coloured silence,
love brands itself into the world, extends its tentacles, and I hear
a crisp, tinny hatching sound –
the vital force of life walking away from its dusty dwelling,
step by step toward reality. Have you parched land,
lodged in the same dream with me, heard it too?
In a flash of lightning, I awaken first,
shedding my spring nectar with raindrops for you.

Soulfulness

The pillow of the world is said to be the deep blue starry sky
above Baghdad, that in legend, Allah will return to every now and then
when he misses the stunning stargazing from Earth.

Isn't it the way they say –
one who fails to tell where he is when hiding in himself
will miss that stars when stepping out?
Or what other way can it be?

Never mind. It only matters
when you see the steady signal of their eternal wisdom.

Stargazing

For two or three centuries
no dreamland could be found on Earth.
Wagons of pioneers dragged broken dreams toward their final rest
in a museum; the struggle between Dr. Jekyll and Mr. Hyde
has been abandoned for years.
Interstellar spaceships, fleet after fleet, emerge through
wormholes, and within a blink
sweep through the pages of a *Cloud Atlas*.

Yesterday Once More

Nothing will come back
from the barrow of night
except for a phantom moon-hare
whose shinbone bore a hole through which you glimpsed
a room full of gem flames sealed in the inmost night
and raised from its warren poised to leap,
through rings of diamond fire.

Yet again, you lifted the binoculars and glimpsed
a phantom ancient moon-hare disgorged
from a deep throat of a sky full of boulders, inferno, sulfur, ice crystals
fleeing as they are fleeting
in a fleeting moment.

Fresh

He aged so much all he had left was voiceless language,
hymns to the Supreme Infinite in his reverent smile.
Such tacit serenity of the moment became his hallmark of expression,
resembling the eternity within Day and Night, Dawn and Twilight,
　　　　over which the Creator rejoices.
Take and fold up this outline and place it alongside starlight
when the first spring breeze blows by. He will take it and blend it into…
the spring is so new, so warm and cerulean,
the youthful joy of spring anew – what a delight!
A verdant world sparkles with ripples of mystic gold.

Let Go

The man caught in the clutches of struggle
floats and sinks, heart relieved or entangled,
a buoy submerged or emerging in a sea of suffering;
Hesperus scintillating before Phospherus to mark the dawn,
the wound gapes, starlight streams down the sacred scar from the dark blue,
leaving no trace of the wandering heart.

The round stone beneath a cared, full moon, rolls downhill…
until the wasteland of pessimism gives up its throne
and the happiness of dawn – a feather of hopefulness
scatters its rosy glow from the struggle. The man
will possess a winged heart, and the heart
will be forged into a tough charioteer of tomorrow, and never waver.

Vision of Yearning

Yearning to climb up the ivy-twined iron railings,
its tiny feet inspect the ground, a giant
dangling shadows in blossom;
the sun exposes everything, the sky cracks,
blue bionic mimicries collapse,
apples tumble; it's time to set off barefoot!
Do voices of cool wind wander in a strange vision,
blow in my face, footprints of light tickle
as silver sweats
overflow a gold paradise?

Shady plants with thorny arms and hands,
moss on one side, pitch-dark door
on another, lead into the motionless stillness.
The giant footprint of night treads
at the edge of the dream, tilting
a corner of the garden you envisioned,
tiny green fruits thrusting,
shyly reflecting every slight silver moonbeam.
Blurs of brightened beams of light,
learning in their humble way
to salvage the imperceptible falling
of this slippery world towards a bottomless abyss.

Autumnal Musing

Like a blade of crabgrass,
the old woman became a fixture at the subway entrance,
over a long winter, a spring, a summer.
Now, autumn has settled,
the woman who crumbles like sandy soil
still holds in her hand tiny flower pots,
mutters, with a trembling voice,
as if squeezed from cracked buildings,
"Flowers for sale..."

On my windowsill,
a small pot of Jewel Flowers has survived three seasons.
It reminds me silently
with its last, plump petals.
"Relax, death has its own clock."

A Beggar with a Skin Disease

In summer,
on the route I take between my workplace and home each day,
is a beggar with a skin disease. I always encounter him,
ceaselessly scratching his dirty body.

I imagined
by the end of that summer
he would be devoured entirely by fester,
then vanish.

The following autumn,
marvellously, he was still wandering
on the path between my workplace and home,
scratching no more.

The merciful autumn wind blew away the summer days
and carried with it his hopelessness.

Copying

Wandering in the post-meridian Lotus Market,
I encountered a circle with a cheerful American woman tourist
and a well-trained Chinese titmouse at the center,
their mouths opened simultaneously
to a one yuan coin:
"Good Boy!"

The titmouse prudently turns down a dime,
and onlookers from different races
offer their sincere praise
at how he replicates, precisely, human traits.

Bird Language

Across from the People's Hospital is a small Bird & Flower Market,
secluded as in a hospital during SARS.

In one of the stores, several sculptural blackbirds
perch idly on tiny branches in their cages
while around their necks a ring of golden hackles
suggest a sort of noble label:
"de" or "von."

From the hospital, several mask-wearing idlers drop by
and listen to the birds' most requested lines:
"Hello" followed by "Welcome, welcome,"
their mouths behind masks of open laughter.

One mouth in the crowd speaks affectedly of the birds' tones,
eyes full of flirting – "Welcome, welcome."

A long silence,
a long gap in the "caw-caw-caw,"
a blackbird abruptly bursts into strange laughter.

When interpreted in human language,
it probably means
"I see you speaking in bird language, you man!"

Source of Form Invention

It's plain to see, the key point of this photo is cuteness,
alluring, yes, so the key point is how instinctively the photographer
raised his camera,
pointed it as a four-year-old Syrian girl.

No one would expect the apparition of the darkness, the terror,
nowhere to hide in the war-ridden towns, it's a curse that penetrates
deep into the marrow. The little girl shot, her hands above her head,
"surrender" to the staring camera lens –
that dark, dark "gun."

No one can imagine that instinctive response,
a pattern recognition established in the instinctive moment
even before she understands how to react emotionally.

Such heart-breaking "action"
invents a pattern of denunciation conspicuous to war's chaos.

The Birth of a Rose

The siren red sky
spans the nightfall

amethyst raindrops fall

the high summer hanging on tips of a tree
cling to a dead green shell-shaped leaf

the plankton of heat swim under a microscope
in clouds, petals of roses wash their faces

Strings break with a sound of ripping cloth

a weird street sprinkler tears off the heat
splashing passersby one by one
hopping like birds on the ground

a girl in a red dress
her body thin as a flower stem
blossoms silently in the spray of droplets

When she awakes
crystal beads of sweat on her skin
make her a rose tinseled in dew

Green Love

Riding on a bicycle, singing in the rain all along her way,
she encounters someone in a dark-green raincoat
and popping out of it is half of a pure young man's face
a flower half-open before her eyes.

A nightmare fallen out of those eyes,
cold-blooded intuition of reptiles.

Many webbed-footed umbrellas,
spiders of colours, crawl in the streets and lanes,
as an earthworm stretches in the rain, longer and longer until it
breaks in two –
two brains headed in opposite directions.

Dancing out of their sky, they are too human.

In the overwhelming posture
of pouring a glass of water,
wet trees meet over the street,
in an arching green fog.

Love Lock

Falling snowflakes and distance gaping between us
are both with tesserae of brightness. Crystalline glitter of ice
depicting its lucid aloofness. From afar, I love you inside me
embracing the shackle of vital heat while "being alive." That day, alone,

winter chained to cold rain, on the Hohenzollernbrücke, I walked into a
    graveyard of locks!
Railings of love locks, popped out one point-in-time, 26.07.1971
a DD-MM-YY before I was born, emerged after checking half the bridge
within the shackle of a love lock, it re-encountered itself:

half retained in the fervent past, beholding the departure of another
a complete time point rising out of years of anonymity and oblivion
revived inside another one calling for attention.
A flint point of time

with its plump, immortal coldness to light up the opaque horn of envisioning...
searching continuously, before getting frozen stiff, and on another lock I found
14.07.1956, a DD-MM-YY before you were born, and now, it's
your turn to stand before it, watching another point-in-time

its purity unfolding, bit by bit, in the fish-belly-white sky,
in the overlay of our visions – a love lock made of two points
        and one missing line
that locks this moment, the memory of love –
etches its name in a door plate with the whole iron bridge held fast,
sealed by all the love locks.

Poetess Pallas Athena

Rather than sex, I write
with the ocean and its raging waves in my womb
looking down
into my empty chalice
and labour in the vastness of Zeus' brilliant brain.

The Drama of Mantra

Rage
turns Durga's heart into an onion
a dew of a fallen tear as huge as a tiger
her spell-casting words
driven by the energy of anger
scurrying such power of completion, with a stupendous thud
that pours out a temple of rats.

Through generations when humans draw nearer to the lightning
a diversity of beliefs spills over the earth:
the mantra is the uncontrollable life infused
in the human utterance of a divine thunderbolt of rage.

Afterwards, by this force in its memory
rage gives birth to a handful of accidental poets.

Fu Hsi Shih

Under a star of distant epochs long ago
comes a shrivelled old woman
a bag is her dress
filled with yellow clay and a thick black clod of clay.

Beneath a row of nearby moons
two children are playing "house"
when the old woman wants to play with them –
the boy frightened enough to cry, the girl crying too
after a second of thought.

The old woman is heartbroken yet tearless;
she is too old to ride a broom and has
to play with the clay inside her bag,
as if a legendary happiness lies within the clay.

Her fingers mold the clay into little people like her, one after another
hanging all over her dress like the flags of nations
until the yellow clay is used up, and only the black clod remains
Her dress is hollow and shrivelled too.

The old woman is happy but fails to laugh.
The snow thickens and deepens until it reaches her lips.
She wonders when the clay-molding happened before...

This time neither she nor any of her little people survive;
the latter, hatched from this thick black clod,
becomes a little person named spirit.

Man Ploughing and Woman Weaving

When a red bridal veil covers the Weaver Girl,
she marries herself to a Persian carpet or a Xuancheng rug.
She starts twisting threads from the morning of this year
and ends in knotting threads at the dusk of another
until she gives birth to a small carpet.

But legend says her husband was a bull
who married a Gnome's daughter, a sallow-faced girl.
The Weaver Girl wonders whether she's the daughter.
Yes, her face is also pale and sallow.
That's none of her business, though,
for she cares more about how, with green crops and cotton linens,
she weaves her predestined life in tradition.

God-creating Movement

In the maze, two football teams
run within the high walls, back and forth, chasing the ball
their eyes alert in the dream
but eventually miss the goal.

Many years later
nobody can remember why they came and what they did here
only a plump, round, dumb primal memory –
like a ball?
Maybe that is their god.

Hence, they settle in the maze
and believe it is from the God's will
that they are to live and feud with others.

Waxing and Waning

Never contented man,
will you only drink the wine of ineffable satisfaction
until its foam overflows in your goblet of happiness?
Oh no, you'd better not.
Once it is in your belly, there is no way to trace its sweetness,
you'll be left with only your spectacle of limp, wild dancing
but no audience will be content with
such a plain performance of inability to please all.
You do know this, don't you?
Only in full bloom, fragrances of fragile branches of the ideal,
cherished by an empty hungry artist,
can lush contentment sigh and spill over
in every enchanting full-moon night.

Matchstick Men

Since then, we shall choose to take our own paths, separately
and be what a single flame could be:
starting a prairie fire of our own,
or kindling distinctive stars alight,
until we all turn into smoldering wicks, drained batteries
when, at a specific moment,
assorted inconveniences dissolve in memories.
People living in limitations wait
for the legendary satori to come,
travel paths open, full of pathos;
not a single silver birch will be forgotten,
nor will every wind riding on a wild horse fade away;
from Forbidden City to the Colosseum, Ganga-nadi-valuka to
        Mount Golgotha,
you are the touch of a will-o'-the-wisp where all things vanish
and the line in which all things are contained.

A Statue of Flying
—talking with Tomaž Šalamun and the Sky

*One day, after translating a Šalamun poem, a big wind still soars outside the window;
the dusk descends gradually. I suddenly find that being in a room on the 16th floor, I
was in the air seeing as one who sees only people but not buildings. So I talked with
Tomaž and the sky…*

I cannot fly, I can only figure out how you fly.
Then, one day, I, the hollow one, unexpectedly flew up
in a rosy dusk, next to a whole day's soaring wind and dust,
the shade of towering pines swayed on the opposite wall of this lit-up night.
One, who watched incessant crowds stream on the busy street, jostling packed
    skyscrapers,
from a room on the 16th floor of a building, beneath
the cool single star in the southwest sky, I was struck by a clarity
in the eye of one who sees a person of flesh and blood
standing on the point of void in the universe,
suspending, meditating, strolling idly, safely, cloaked in love's delusion,
treading in the airy tragedy, expressing a hollow-beauty lyric:
could we still hold dreams of the future clearer than the memory of travelling,
if only being on the boundless sea, beyond sight of dry land
merged sea and sky but without gods to shed their mercies,
being under golden clouds with rosy fingers but pointing to no places,
being in immensity and endlessness but with no thing to depend on?
Could we still appreciate every beautiful detail cherished by the world
where every aspect deserves a careful second look?
Could you still insist on abundant willpower and stride forward singing
    triumphantly:

speedy flying saves more effort, higher one, saves more labour?
could you still boldly blow the melancholy ocean into the prevailing wind
    and announce:
you are full of hunger enveloping a sky that never could be fed?

Rose Garden

A drizzle falls on each headstone,
and for a long time does not pour down into minutes, seconds,
nor hours, months, years. Time is of no use.
The cemetery is immersed in the bottomless pit of autumn rain,
leafless branches tracing veins of night;
stone sculptures of angels, children, urns, carvings…
increase and blend in the promised land of nothingness
turn into one common name: death
a pseudonym of *Il nome della rosa.*

Winding graveyard, endless path, it rains
in the passionate symbol garden of the tranquil world.
Browsing among tombstone pages of this memorial book
wandering visitors are spellbound
as every letter spills over from the tranquility;
detached from the context of the world's stone language,
symbols fall away into life or death
and lament the homeland with no means of return.

In Powazki Cemetery, I made one cautious step
closer to the stone forbidden zone of nihilism
plunged into the vast unknown!
The entire Earth rises from this meditation
and becomes a colossal dark rose garden.

Memory Disk Formatting

She sat at the bank, soulless water flowing
like a collapsed river levee
like an ideal losing its radiance
like a love elegy losing its rhythm
like a hard drive stripped of its memory
or a room that was vacated
leaving only self-denying lines of walls.

Favour Lost

—modelled from a Scottish ballad

My suede jacket is dog's skin,
clumps of fluffy brown pompoms, so well-arranged
so well-fit, as the old maxim:
when the skin is gone, where can the hair grow?
Gone are my beloved childhood
and my suede jacket.
The dog I secretly asked to take my food
in those blessed years
took away my jacket, my grain.

Pearls from a Tainted Oyster

You, protector of yourself
cherished of yourself.
You, the tainted oyster
the pearl you made from your own body.
You made because you must love yourself, let weariness fall away.
Love yourself, in the name of everlasting bravery.
Even if they pluck off your feathers,
you are still you—a macaw
and You grow new plumage from your own courage!
Even if they cut off your musk, snake gall, antelope horn
you will come back and repair yourself,
never a submissive pessimist, a waverer,
but endure all and face up to the full menu of the world helplessness.

Epitaph

I only want to go home and lie deep
like lying on the waveless bottom, full fathom five
like a lotus seed buried in a coal bed for a thousand years
like a virus settled in the abyss without a ghost.
People,
please don't disturb me with your fire
the fire that destroys all
the fire that falls with darkness into ashes
before my dusty, cadaverous face.

In the Chilly Air, All You Touch Is Iron

Shush! Don't speak of the infinite animals
planted in my dark garden they one, two...
haven't existed in people's eyes.
All you see and seen only by you
is an iron density; what is bestowed on you
is your own burden. Your eyesight,
your hearing, your burdened sickly
senses are all watching:
each and every garden inside the shape
of the dark-starry-sky-animals I herd...
So much glory that one would bow to
submit one's self before God's throne, the tick-tick
of glimmering drops out of melting ice...
In the chilly air, all you touch aches in you like iron,
solid iron. The Complete You,
the Indifferent You, the Unattainable You...
I know your willingness, which has settled
in my poem of tears...

Feeding

You are still a boy,
cherishing a boy's dream and love,
whisking endlessly in the bowl of worldly sadness
the savory jam of fantasy.
You spread the jam on the steel surface
of the sliced bread of earthly living,
and feed adults with gusto
to inspire a continual growth
but not a rapid aging.

The overflowing cornucopia,
though worn, torn, damaged,
is still pouring the incessant tiger-growl of love.

The Cost of Love

This little boy has round grapes in his eyes.
That little girl has cherry lips.
If you love me, three sparkling stars I'll see.
If you do not, a deer limps on his sore fore-hoof
and star-rain will pour down.
Three hundred stars I saw that night,
hooves tossing in my stomach
aching until the crack of dawn.

Rondo

"Passing Years" is a folk song leaving sadness in one's chilled chest;
there comes a moment when no horse will pass by
on the vast plain of heart, but must turn its head and cock its ears to listen:
a simple melody like the mountain you gazed at as a child,
melting into the twilight and fading away at the end of the road while you
    look back.
All mournful songs of separation, death, roaming, and exile
come from and drift about with the ancient ballads;
the beginning of the world also could find its shelter in your body,
could ascend the ladder you would have climbed in the wind,
could follow up your flourishing or impoverished years, loudly or silently.
At a moment when the mind stretches into a far afield,
you hear the folk song that was heard and will be heard
by an ancestor or descendant who forced and will be forced to the chill
    to retreat
with a stove burning to fire their souls out of the dark days.

Nascita Di Venere

Out of the sea you arise, amidst the empathy bestowed by the spray,
fantasy borne in brine, a seashell, diamonded by
longings for the mortal world, ascending from the spiral spout
of a fin whale, clouds full of grandeur, cutting through
a liquid crystal world where the sound of water splashing like that
of rustling plastic foil, echoing in ears multiple space-times away;
appearances of the world dancing ceaselessly, achievements
of God's math and kinetics embedded in spirals of the conch,
one force of the initial thrusts gently loosened its grip
from such a long alert combat-ready rein of the world,
a carelessness fell, like a reversed spiral spout of the whale, back into the sea,
crashing into a first-sight love between its surging floods and the shell,
have you felt it—the weight of home-returning waves burdening you?
(In the standard version of the myth,
Cronus throws out a huge flint-bladed sickle
of time and castrates his father Uranus, the great creator with wild fantasy,
spewing waves of pure sperm that give birth to Venus, goddess
of love and beauty,
who is engraved on all minds everywhere.)

Inside multiple space-times, a maternal body—in a blurred dream
fattened up by the feeling of defectiveness,
a fearful wreck of nativity, besmeared with blood,
draws itself out of the conch—a female corporeality
still owning an elegant elongated neck, disproportionate,
heeling to the left, with further wrenching, turning head,
biting the navel cord off… She, a wrecked ship, lies

dreadfully on the sea beach like this. In my dream,
a different reality relieves me, my face breezed by the salty-fishy
sea wind: olfaction received first the sense of being rescued,
I followed behind a man, a beam of light, whose upper torso
misaligns with the lower part, who seems to
have been met somewhere before. A light refraction
under the sea surface illuminates a garden full of
conches, and within each and every sea cradle lies every
soft you and me—console itself, with blessings,
striving to grow and all wounds will find salvation.

From afar, white lateen sails of a galleon are bulging like shells,
so realistic and sublime as paintings of the Renaissance.
Botticelli knows clearly the divinity and the humanity and reconstructs
a corner of the ocean, on a Tridacna gigas, brings forth
an immortal goddess who owns the will of beauty that elevates all,
long blonde hair as clouds, hands concealing her private parts,
such a graceful way, elegant neck elongated disproportionately.

(While my alienated version of the myth re-narrates:
Aphrodite does not ascend on the giant clam, she struggles
and crawls through the narrow spiral jagged path
of a tiger cowry, the free wayfarer on the sea of desire,
leaves something inside the cowry, not dragged out in time,
but a newborn as me, does not fathom out the complicated
world and the missing self, but knows not what was left.

Since then, she goes all over the earth and oceans, living in
coition, when that big head struggles hard into the mouth
of her cowry time and again, she always desires to recall
the precious property she left in her origin. She seems to find it, almost,
yet, in the blank seas of aphrodisia climax, it will, every time,
slip and fall into the infinite dark blue of the vast starry sky,
such a doomed Sisyphus in the sea!)

Pandora, Pandora

As Socrates died, he said: "To live - that means to be sick
a long time: I owe Asclepius the Savior a rooster."
— FRIEDRICH NIETZSCHE, *Twilight of the Idols*

I have four stomachs, and enough coarse gravel borrowed
from the rooster, so, that's why I could digest
today's world? You just owe me one rooster,
why do you wake in me so much déjà vu—
all over land, and teeming the ocean, a raven, that raven,
flying and peering for me! The world eternally
stretches its fiery whirls, I am forever, the dark coke
of apocalypse? Salvation retreats continually in history,
moth, the noctilucent moth, dissipated fire-ashes and gold powder,
where will you go? The multitude diseases of my crowded river,
the thin figures of maids in hometown festivals, I am sober
so very sober. That being the case, well, then,
there should be something, an alluring scarlet sindoor
deep down on my heart, why I could never recall
where that tiny HOPE is? I get on the bus, watching
on screen the replication of human madness: wild singing and dancing,
bathing in laser shining. Those of clay awaken,
weight of living still pressing harshly on their chests, what is the worth
    of life? You
blindly tolerate every worthless lie, throughout every stage of life.
To pump desires into performance, yet performance fails to anoint the arts.
To be what you're not is your only true reality,
what's invented is your poker face, or even hands,

a chap's, the hand eking out a living by mending tires,
facing me, stretching out in the newspaper picture,
with a look aging at 50 years older, rooster-claw-like fingers
curling up in dust, in the pitch darkness of hopelessness
enduring the never arrival of dawn. Intolerable reality—
that a human being unhappy is still due to the fact that he knows not
his happiness, really? Endurance, then, is a huge secret
or a mask, hiding entwined love and hate, horrid the morbid.
Mercy on yourself! Let love break out, make hate melt, have mercy on
souls of the lonely, the sufferers, the diseased. To die,
all of us will die soon, very soon, what takes over you,
what will be you. Your mortal flesh is fully occupied by boredom,
so is your life, your world. Stories still performed are only
in the non-human world, without orders nor chronicles,
ignoring ideologies and labours. Changeability of All changes,
    the huge bell of canopy,
a stud-star in the coat of Asclepius is bursting apart, the charming star
is in the Ophiuchus alluring us in this way under our nose? Thousands of
    years later,
the star winking at us — it would be the closest neighbor of our Earth.
    Will Orion,
its Guiding stars, Jacob's cane reflected on the location
of Great Pyramid of Khufu, point the way for blade runners to attack
    spaceships?
The one struggled against the inferno at the jaws of death, his moments
    had been erased,
slipping away from time, as tears melting in the rain.
Pure existence or no existent. Betelgeuse on the shoulder of the Orion

would collapse lively in front of us. Still, wisdom is considered to be
    knowing one's ignorance,
the recognition that Socrates' gods mattered the most and kept to themselves
    alone.
Still, choosing hope is the beginning of hope,
a rooster's crowing tangled in the memory, offers
a dawn ritual of hope for the long sick living.

Primacy

Holding a fishing rod, a little boy felt a nibble for the first time.
The nature "to possess" hasn't budded, the fish at-hand was alive and kicking;
Little boy astounded, pulling the rod
for a little while, being at a loss with eyes fixed, overwhelmed,
turned his head and asked, "What is its name"
"Name it however you wish," his papa said.
Engaged in a linguistic theophany, the boy named the fish "freedom"!
Genius is always there, despite some hesitancy.
The boy was afraid to begin: to touch or not to touch,
that is a question; the possibility of touching "freedom"
merely lies in the nature of imagining; the boy's little heart and eyes timidly
worked together, fulfilling the touch!
"Freedom" was then put back into the water...

At the end of the long fishing rod, an empty hook
shining in the sun, like the silver minnow of a maxim:
the interestedness of possessing is the younger brother
and the playfulness of being amazed is the older.

Evolution

The two ravens of Odin both grow long feathers,
one longer, the other shorter,
and both feathers are not black, but
one glowing red, the other green. In the legend,
the red-glowing comes from the Sun, while the green
is not from the Moon, but from the emerald,
a family heirloom of raven's grandmother, inherited
and swallowed by every generation. That's why
the green-glowing feathers are never bright, but have almost a faint sadness.
One day, Odin's ravens –
Huginn and *Muninn (Thought* and *Memory)*
in the white glowing spouted from a lunar flare,
dream the same wolf nightmare: grilled in the fire
of howls stockpiled by wolves through generations,
bit by bit, piece by piece, torn up, and decaying into
a distributed entropy of colours from bright to dark, here comes
Literature, History, Philosophy.

Architectural Modelling

You light up a thousand-fold brightness and the lamp
of the tabernacle in my heart.
An encircling, swirling, building brightness of spirit
embraces summer splendour, greets
the future vastness and its haziness; no one knows
its composition:
both water and wind, fire and clay,
morning and night, salt and sugar,
hence no one knows how it will dissipate.

It was built according to the law of truly large numbers, whirlpools
of humanity, labour and rest: on a coastal beach,
peaceful as somewhere east of Eden,
people, like me,
witness its expanse from the Earth below to the sky above:
from a tiny letter to a flying star,
from the interior of a lotus to its blessed wet, sweet, fragrance;
sea floor pavements mirror the transgressed green world,
reflect the innocent looks of those invisible,
from two sides of the world, to behold
the open heart of each and every daybreak, the horizon,
radiating the unsurpassed splendor of a rosy dawn,
opening the celestial clam.

Capture

The granary of illumination is filled with grains of luminosity
and the densest brilliant cluster are the capital cities below –
from high above the curtain of night, the astronaut holds the moment
and bends his camera lens,
rotating the Earth along its green blockade of stratosphere:
Iberian Peninsula, the Sinai, Eurasia,
while over the white ocean gallops the emerald bronco of aurora borealis,
a corona of music, an eerie green-steel flooding the planet's rim...

Next to the astronaut, a rare eagle-eye
of originality captures fleeting glimpses:
the light-eating animal,
the diurnal behemoth in the act of beginning
as it protrudes its anteater sticky tongue with hooks
that harvest every grain of brightness.

Advent

... I pluck'd a hollow reed,
... I made a rural pen
            —WILLIAM BLAKE, "Introduction to the Songs of Innocence"

Hung on your horns
were songs interdependent with you.

The humming wreath round your neck turned sallow
beneath circles of slackness which hid your dehydrated body.

My poor old insane Pan
I saw you pluck a hollow reed
lips quivering
before uttering my name in your memory – Syrinx
I had turned into the pen in your hand.

Your dim old eyes didn't lie to you
the land is barren
on places you've walked
the stubble of withered grass pricks your feet.

From afar, rows of thinking reed
reproduce asexually a printed world.

The wind blew away songs on your horns
you listened to the crisp snaps of dry petals fading away
a sense of déjà vu.

You went wild for an instant, jumping up to chase them
and were gone after them, never to return.

Generations later
submerged in the noises of printing machines
my rationality fell into sleep.

Dream droops its rosy hands, one finger pointing to the east, one to the west
    ...
and one to the ancient master –
abruptly I run into your last stuttering wild singing.

The Orchard of Memory

So intertwined! I am watching myself in the orchard
of my body, a gardener and fruit trees, eventually
in its full bloom, plinky-plunky, fetishes and fire-breathing monsters
are all climbing trees with their copper limbs; the soprano flute of branches
ascending all its way up, further than the eyes can see...

I have no more Atman to lie within!

In the theatre of eyes, on stage is *Appearance of Mountains and Rivers*;
drifting towards me are brown wet clouds,
a grain of cloud clay in hand, seeds of angels in the soft palm;
right at the place of my heart—a glowing empty furnace,
a tiny verdure pops out, driven by the abyss of heat,
soon, in the blowing of wind, burgeoning a row of radishes,
a boy is screaming inside my throat:
   "Mum, Mum, look, look,
radishes are huge, huge as a god."

I have a god to live within.

Silver apples of moons,
gold apples of suns
galloping, on the planets orbits in orchard, standing
in the giant mouth of ○, the line-shape magician
is huffing and puffing, disgorging rays of light waves, amongst which, I am
a small shining surging-out sturgeon, a little bad shaped,
yet apparently overjoyed, leading waves head shaking and tail wagging,

joys overrunning, seen from afar
an ineffable wavy eye reflection hanging high above the sky.

I have a vision and eye-light to reside within.

At the bottom of a fathomless pond, the drum door leading to a
    myriad secret beings,
an ivy vine of ancient drum rhythms entwining my feet,
    the immortality of lyricism
keeps climbing and growing upwards along me, the giant dream tree drumming,
my foliage trembling, in the resounding of a timpani bang,
Ms. "Beetle-juice" arising, adorned with her necklace
of cowries, benzene rings, erecting in the center of flaming sufferings,
nearby her husband, Orion, thundering against her,
the solar wind of Betelgeuse blowing harder and harder,
the juice of beetles, elytra, shells keep effusing.

I bear a fiery dream locked in deep rocks.

At the gash of spiritual earth of transfigured mountains and rivers
arises an agate-colored dream serpent, the tail-devourer Ouroboros,
a glowing creature devouring time figures one by one on the watch face,
refracting the light spectrum relived out of many a generation
I am the Alpha and Omega, "the first and the last, apart from me
    there is no God."

Writings of memory extending, a green giant serpent
licks the earth and flows to the sea, with flared orchards

and rose trees on its back; a flower branch of horses,
clicking and clacking, melts into sperm whales.

The Paradise of the Solar System

An idealist fixes his gaze
at the high noon sun and sees conclusively
the paradise of the solar system.

In *Civitas Solis*, countless streets radiate
from the central plaza of the Sun;
within every arm of sunlight,
lives a dazzling, lanky shadow of gods and creatures;
brilliant spots that blind every long gaze, strut in exultation,
circling the glorious body of creation;
up and down, lights and shadows, flashing and reflecting,
these good riders are so absorbed in this identity-switch tarot,
yet whichever card is turned
illumines the celestial light and tells the score.

Shining drops of sweat flow down
the forehead and naked flesh
of the idealist bathing in the high noon sun,
flowing into countless radiating streets.

That Line

THAT LINE, first emerging on the horizon,
extending through ups and downs, stretching leisurely, relaxed, unwittingly
arches its back and glances at the vastness and beyond
from where the legend might be told: on the roof of the world, stands
a young mountain a hundred million years old.
THAT LINE wonders in a trance,
whom are they talking about?

THAT LINE crawls out of the midday ocean,
a rolling coastline rimmed with a lace of waves
carrying the memory of thunder and lightning ripping away heavy clouds,
casting occult roars from the dazzling, fiery sun;

THAT LINE, by moonlight, climbs up the cities' skylines,
uplifting church steeples, creeping on temple eaves and walls,
huddles as block of skyscraper, scattered bright stars high in the canopy
are well-known to him. THAT LINE,
standing higher, seeing farther, going to
places higher and farther, the starry firmament,
determines to set out for eternal infinity…

THAT LINE leaps over the "Pillars of Creation" in the Eagle Nebula,
and finds itself high as four light-years away, forming the outline
of the first Pillar, EGGs – incubators of stars cracking
one by one, along its majestic bulk;
THAT LINE stretches over Carina Nebula, the hull bottom nebula,
fifty light years wide at its bilge

within the nebulosity of star-forming energy, the past embracing the future,
death following birth, gorgeous Eta Argus, eyes wide open,
watching its doomed failure to hold the Great Eruption as its sides,
the line will break, is about to break…

Quit it! THAT LINE flees quickly, gleefully,
tastes the ferocity of nature, the rapture, a supernova
seen by earthlings one thousand years ago
as it exploded vividly in deep space millions of years before,
whose absurd scattering still fly to us this day;
THAT LINE that passes through the Crab Nebula it once crawled out of,
rotates above a pulsar within,
its robust long arms flailing giddily;
THAT LINE feels its youth, so blessed a youth
that Earthlings say:
so far death is unknown.

THAT LINE, begetter of all forms,
its youthful heart fears no chaos even in the chaos of a black hole,
an astonishing glut of amassed matter;
THAT LINE twisting twice, leaving a gas-dust disc
bearing all scattered remnants hastily, extrudes through the black hole in M87;
a jet of ejected matter as long as five thousand light years, a lengthy, legendary
journey forward of rays, the myriad of unknowns in the eternal vacuum,
escaped the point where destruction of all forms occurs;

the palpitated memory engenders a lingering fear,
henceforth, THAT LINE, either sets as a pillar, a mainstay

or sails untrammelled into the vast, stellar-aggregated cosmos,
shuns its POINT only, in the unique "singular point,"
where there is no past, present, future, or lights, and all is nothing,
a cosmic loophole, invisible pinpoint
funnelling and condensing into oblivions
all doomed imaginings and their creatures that sail in.
THAT LINE incarnates in every form, thrashing in the revelry
of the invisible sole inhabitant on the center stage of the vast galaxy,
stars being barged, swerved, thrown off at high speed,
such a mania of cosmic monodrama…

THAT LINE senses something moving slightly in the dream
within a breath it takes every ten-thousand years
in a half-sleep disturbed by exhaustion and restlessness;
THAT LINE sees the farther stars from itself
the faster they move toward a red light more distant
seeming to have realized in the dream THAT LINE
cries of its certain invisible fate…
The dream of Redshift – so bursts the name when it awakes, which is
caught by a dream-catcher on Earth and recorded
on a page of some science log:
there is a cosmic straightedge named Hubble's Law –
a line that never gets lost in time,
and measures the expanding universe with time as it goes by…

THAT LINE penetrates the secret of time and space, knows well
the ending of everything, the prime driver of the cosmic expending event,
the unseen panel of masters, the pervasive dark energy
that will ultimately win over the forces of gravity and atom aggregation

where only two words are written by the restless law –
"To Die!"
THAT LINE, born of the Big Bang, will eventually
be torn apart by the Big Rip into numerous disperse points…
The end of absolute quietus.
Earthlings know the miasma of it: the beginning and the ending are both points;
yet somehow earthlings know everything begins in points and so do they end,
hence come the names beginning and end.

And now, through the infinite generations
THAT LINE, the entity of all form,
after every Good Night ending on TV, lies idly
amidst flakes in the background of cosmic microwaves
flickering as reflected shimmers of gossamer.

AFTERWORD
by XIA KEJUN

ON THE POETRY OF ZHAO SI: INVENTOR
OF NEW MYTHS AND HER NAME OF CINNABAR MOLE

The writing of great and solemn poetry has always been under the vast and deep dome of myth and history, under the never inscrutable but strict scrutiny of gods. The Muse of Poetry expects a new way of ventriloquism to be reborn from her abdomen; it needs poets to gaze at the stars anew, deciphering the iconography of constellations, weaving the light beams of memories, stepping into the realm of truly large numbers, turning over mental imagery within whirlpools, connecting heaven and earth, ghosts and gods – just as Zhao Si writes in her poem "Architectural Modelling," her mode of poetic composition:

> *from a tiny letter to a flying star,*
> *from the interior of a lotus to a blessed wet sweet fragrance;*
> *water floor tiles mirroring the transgressed green world,*
> *reflecting the innocent looks of those invisible,*
> *from two sides of the world, we see each*
> *open heart of every daybreak on the horizon,*
> *radiating the unsurpassed splendor of rosy dawn in the celestial clam.*

Among other contemporary Chinese poems, hardly can we find works with such rich and complex, mysterious yet multicoloured images, that could boldly embrace time and space. Zhao's poetry opens both sides of the world, from forming the *eigentlich* (German for actuality) reality to the superimposing moments of mythic imagination. During this process, the original divine power of words is triggered.

In one of her essays on poetics, "Notes on Searching for the Individual Voice Poetics and Others," Zhao Si writes: "Having doubted the routes and orientations Chinese contemporary poetry has taken, sometimes I have to turn to the most powerful poetry resources – myths, which is the typical model of poetry thinking. Poetry is rooted in myths, in the deep layers of human psychology, in the words bursting from when souls encounter *das Ungeheuer*, the monster. Poetic material other than that are just side issues."(p. 243)[*]
That's why we often find in her poems the rewritings and transformations of Western even worldwide myths and legends, for which she composes a special Metamorphoses in her poetry atlas. An entry into mythology - a primeval symbolic space, is also an entry into an original field of experience where exists great expeditions; the poet becomes a great transformer, renaming and retransforming primeval scenarios or archetypal lives, through which the poet carries the genealogy of great poetry within her. More than that, Zhao Si also introduces primeval scenarios into daily life, creating surreal feelings and illusions of time reversal. Like that in Benjamin's concept "dialectic image," such a dialectic and synthetic modernity makes a sudden integration and explosive *polymerization* (the connection of individual molecules in the process of creating polymers) between ancient and current experiences, generating an amazing spiritual transformation. In one of her masterpieces, "Pandora, Pandora," Asclepius, the god of medicine in ancient Greek mythology – reborn in modern scenarios as a healer in Zhao's rewriting – witnesses the modern chaotic world and the deprivation of human souls. He offers a soliloquy on grief, anguish, accusation, and sympathy, yet insists that out of desperation

[*] The page numbers in parentheses refer to the book *Disappearing, Recalling* by Zhao Si (Writers Publishing House, Beijing, 2016), except for p.184 and p.185 which come from the "Postscript" for *Shade of Eternity: Selected Poems of Lebioda* (Shandong Publishing House of Literature and Art, Jinan, 2017).

and indicating there is still the possibility of "the beginning of hope" through "choosing hope."

To interlace and superimpose images also brings out the awareness of the mythic origin and its mystery even in our daily lives. This mysterious experience from ancient myths to daily life is another discovery by Zhao Si of one more distinctive field, on which she writes in another item of Notes: "I am often staying at the verge between dreaming and wakening, when many lines arrive automatically in this way." (p. 242) That's another state, a field mingled with dreams and the awakening hidden deep in the unconscious memory (mémoire involontaire in Proust and Benjamin), where a poet will accidentally press the poetry code switch concealed within words. In this way, the poet calls us to dive into our own memory reservoir, because these words "wrapped by the intensity of the soul abyss, would never be gushed out and metamorphose into a poem until they find a poet who finds out the soul power sources." (p. 243) The vision brought by this depth is of a natural mystique; mystery only befalls at a high level of cognition. The mastery of the maker who creates your dreams is greatly beyond your imagination when you are sober. Frustrated by this dream master as you might be, you should still bear in mind the shoelaces of dreaming so that the shoes on your feet bring you to the solidity of poetry. That is where Zhao Si's poetry has been moving towards inventing "things of mystique and marginal consciousness in time as well as the self-knowledge reflected within." (p. 278) "Marginal consciousness in time" is the origin of poetic mystique.

Besides the "mystique" of "myths," Zhao Si also tries to rebuild the poetic "mystique" of "sanctity." She draws critical appraisals of the poets she has translated or reflected on: "Adonis is a poet of the primary variety, and the tone he takes is god-like" (p. 184); while the Slovenian poet, Tomaž Šalamun, is a strong contemporary poet, who "puts his location of speaking prior to the apotheosized gods, mainly at the place of apotheosized-to-be gods in the period of 'being wild' before the coming of Jesus Christ......" (p. 185). As a contrast, Zhao Si holds that the speaking location of most contemporary Chinese poets stay as "human," or even "all-too-human." Obviously, she wants to surpass this kind of limitation, and in some her poems chooses the way of sacred experiences. Her reminiscence and poetic imprinting of those lost things are definitely evident in her efforts to step into the sacred palace, making them sacred relics, organizing the poem "into a chorus" in the tone of invisible angels, and releasing her poetic metamorphosis.

Hardly can we find another poet in China like Zhao Si who is able to lift the curse imposed on lives with her vast twofold imagination of "myths" and "sanctity." Poetry, through its history, has always been applied to break the curse hanging over our feelings, and our need to dispel rage and sadness. It is also Zhao Si's intention, when she reforms the primitive images of myths and then turns them into conceptualized words, that she captures an unconscious dream flux. As in "Evolution," the two ravens of Odin Huginn and Muninn (Thought and Memory) decay into entropy of Literature, History, Philosophy in the nightmare of grilling in the fire of time-wolves' howls. This poem appears in the episode "Inherited Secrets" in her book *Disappearing, Recalling* in which she describes the full awareness of the mentioned intention. As an illusionist, through constantly re-writing primitive images, persistently transforming elementary forms, and condensing poetic events of history, Zhao Si creates the poetess l'histoire des mentalites, where she performs the poet's *Beruf* (profession) of imparting the god of wisdom, Athena, to be reborn as a "Poetess Pallas Athena."

This is the "Orchard of Memory" established by Zhao Si, in which the flowing imagination babbles and gurgles in ceaseless amazement:

I have a God to live within.

...

At the bottom of a fathomless pond, the drum door leading to a
  myriad secret beings,
an ivy vine of ancient drum rhythms entwining my feet,
the immortality of lyricism
keeps climbing and growing upwards along me, the giant
dream tree drumming, my foliage trembling, in the resounding of
  a timpani bang,
Ms. "Beetle-juice" arising, adorned with her necklace
of cowries, benzene rings, erecting in the center of flaming sufferings,
nearby her husband, Orion, thundering against her,
the solar wind of Betelgeuse blowing harder and harder,
the juice of beetles, elytra, shells keep effusing.

Such imagination of life is peculiar to "femaleness" which spurts from the sacred matrix and superimposes the transformed female world of Borges and is eventually branded by a special individual name.

Poetry is naming and thus also an art of names. Zhao Si (Zhao4) is an "allonymous" name, a name with a number, a glorified name, the name of the rose, which dates back within a genealogy of myths. The name could also be a Betelgeuse (which in Chinese is associated with the number 4), whose pronunciation is quite the same as that of "beetle juice" in English – a noble woman's name in Mayan Civilization. Zhao once told me that it was this interesting similarity of pronunciation that brought forth the latter half of the stanza in "The Orchard of Memory," which once again proves her originality is rooted in language sources similar to those from which the ancients created myths. More than that, she acquires inspiration codes not only in her mother tongue. Contemporary poetry is actually hybridized, partly by language translation, and is woven into the mixed imaginary re-construction of life. Ever since T.S. Eliot and James Joyce, the great literature of creating has entered into a hybrid re-writing. "Si" with the meaning "four" in Chinese can also refer to the four directions in ancient China, hinting at the transformation of Four Elements or the bounce of echoes surrounded off four bare walls. As "the center of flaming sufferings" described in "The Orchard of Memory," poetry is like that serpent, the tail-devourer Ouroboros, possessing self-sufficiency. Zhao Si intends to endow her poetry with the absolute self-sufficiency of words, as the God of "the Alpha and the Omega, the first and the last" in the Bible. This self-sufficient serpent is of agate-colour. Its scales correspond to the figures on a watch face, refracting the light spectrum with the God's words – an illusory green giant serpent with rose trees on its back like flower branches of horses. This illusory vision glorifies the name of Zhao Si.

In "Pandora, Pandora," the first half of the poem is a re-establishment of the poetic birth of the poet:

> I have four stomachs, and enough coarse gravel borrowed
> from the rooster, so, that's why I could digest
> today's world? You just owe me one rooster,
> why do you wake in me so much déjà vu –
> all over land, and teeming the ocean, a raven, that raven,
> flying and peering for me! The world eternally
> stretches its fiery whirls, I am forever, the dark coke
> of apocalypse? Salvation retreats continually in history,
> moth, the noctilucent moth, dissipated fire-ashes and gold powder,
> where will you go? The multitude diseases of my crowded river,

the thin figures of maids in hometown festivals, I am sober
so very sober. That being the case, well, then,
there should be something, an alluring scarlet sindoor
deep down on my heart. I could never recall
where that tiny HOPE is? I get on the bus, watching
on screen the replication of human madness: wild singing and dancing,
bathing in laser shining. Those of clay awaken,
weight of living still pressing harshly on their chests, what is the worth of
    life? You
blindly tolerate every worthless lie, throughout every stage of life.
To pump desires into performance, yet performance fails to anoint
    the arts.

One needs "four stomachs" – vaster than the giant stomach in the imaginations of American poets in early Industrial Age – though with four stomachs, one cannot digest the tremendous love and hate, solitude and suffering of this world, then, where is the HOPE? When the Pandora's box opens, despair and hope are flying simultaneously into the world and it is for this reason the poem repeatedly asks why we are facing the mingling of hope and despair and needs the guiding star of the mythic constellation. With Betelgeuse not collapsing, C-rays glittering at the nearby the star gate of chaos, moments submerge into time-torrents, as tears melting in the rain. The poet still believes that facing the retrogression of history, the poetic imagination remains possibly the path to salvation, whether it is a "pure existence or non existence."

Confronted and ceaselessly devoured by the fate of individuals, poetry writing, in the modern sense, is no more than the persistent births of individual poetic lives reborn again and again. This is the life of the politics of birth and the strength of the poetic imagination. In the case of the world being drawn into immense fiery whirls, the poet keeps the alluring scarlet imprint of hope on her heart, or Cinnabar Mole, just as the most concealed writing of the poet herself is also the most beautiful mark in Chinese Art, a mark which has been converted into a self-mark of contemporary poetry and a mystical trill of words. This is the real signal of HOPE.

Therefore, Zhao Si re-invents a sort "previous life," and meanwhile expands the image of her life as it existed so long ago, secret in its dissemination and effusion of the name.

The art of poetry writing for Zhao Si is based on a mingled imagination which depends on the precise generating power of words. This power takes hold of the inner instinctive harmony of sounds and meanings while applying hybrid imaginations from heterogeneous cultures. This mingled imagination accepts the ecstasy of deities but also possesses the reflective thinking ability at depth, which has coalesced painstakingly from "divine madness" and "clarity of expression" by poets since Hölderlin. How has Zhao Si accomplished this? Knowing the beauty of repetition in Chinese classical literary rhyming works, she retrieves rhyming and restraint of elegant ancient Chinese. She also realizes that repetitive words have the rhymes born with the connection between Chinese words and the magic power created by the inner calling of the Chinese language. Meanwhile, modern Chinese language also demands that she restore the classical aesthetic flavour within its twists and turns of writing when encountering its own breakage in modern times. What Zhao Si has done is to renew and regenerate Chinese poetic syntaxes through her brilliant wording and phrasing ability with sentences, and by a return to the classic elegance of the language while keeping modern fragmentation domed under the myths of the imagination, which have long been lacking in Chinese culture.

Power and eloquence are never absent in Zhao Si's poetry: familiarity with historical allusions increases image saturation while a softness and a beauty make details striking and touching. When reading Zhao's poems, I am always amazed by the status that breeds her poetic imagination which indicates a poet with both experiences in her extensive travelling abroad and the imagination dissociated from her experiences. Her wide vision deep into world myths and human history as a whole mingles with classically delicate feelings embedded in ancient Chinese literary traditions possessed only by Chinese women.

I can feel a romanticism that mixes both post-modernity and multiple modernities, for she knows well the secret of spiritual heritance and owns the gift of fuguing poetic techniques. Enlightenment is brought forth with the dreamy addition of myth archetypes, giant leaps of symbolic scenarios, automatic superimposings of surreal visions, perspectives acquired from depth, immortal illusions regained from death, firmness against chill, dim tree shadows that resist aging – all attributes associated with the offspring of Muses.

Zhao Si's words and syntax are changeable and various but maintain neat rules, express a poetic and precise logic motivated by a powerful imagination in words. This is a real polyphonic writing of mixed voices. Her powerful imagination reappears from the lost things in nature, from in the forms of future memories, expressions of love salvaged from their demise, carved from the sacred relics of a hissing haunting serpent, out of a bow's reflection, searching for permanent memory from all lost things so that her poetry can access a depth that could only be delivered in the sacred voice of the soul.

NOTES TO THE POEMS

"Stargazing." The novel referenced, *Cloud Atlas,* is a narrative of interconnectivity between times, places, and individuals. The novel was written by David Mitchell and became the 2004 film of the same title.

"Yesterday Once More." The title is borrowed from a song by the 1970s brother and sister musical duo, The Carpenters, who recorded a popular song, "Yesterday Once More."

"Autumnal Musing." The title references a type of common titles in Chinese classical poetry, for instance, "Eight Octaves on Autumnal Musings" by the Tang Dynasty poet, Du Fu.

"Bird Language." The term can be taken literally, but can also mean "to talk nonsense," "to talk gibberish," or "to talk in a foreign language the listener will not understand."

"Poetess Pallas Athena." In Greek mythology, Pallas Athena, also known simply as Athena, was the goddess of wisdom and ideas. In the story of her birth she is said to have leapt fully armed with shield, helmet, and spear from the head of her father, Zeus.

"The Drama of Mantra." Durga, a goddess in Hindu culture and beliefs, is the guardian of the Karni Mata Temple, which is known as the temple of rats in Rajasthan, India.

"Fu His Shih." In the Chinese myth, "Tuan Tu Zao Ren," by Fu His Shih, the action of "kneading clay" known as Tuan Tu means to make people out of clay and bears a connection to the Biblical concept of God making man out of dust and animating him by "breathing into" or "inspiring" the inanimate dust.

"Man Ploughing and Woman Weaving." A Xuancheng carpet was renowned in ancient China for the craftsmanship and delicacy of its design. The poem is based on a famous Chinese legend of a cowherd and a weaving maid where the man could be, according to linguistic allusions (re-written by the poet), both a man and a bull.

"Matchstick Man." The final lines of the poem are a paraphrase of words from Percy Bysshe Shelley's "On Life" where Shelley states, "Each is at once the center and the circumstance; the point to which all things are referred, and the line in which all things are contained."

"A Statue of Flying." Tomaž Šalamun (1941-2014), mentioned in the epigraph, was arguably the leading voice in Slovenian poetry during his lifetime, and had a major impact on Eastern European verse.

"Rose Garden." *Il nome della rosa* (*The Name of the Rose*) is the title of a novel by Umberto Ecco. Powazki Cemetery is in Warsaw, Poland.

"Favour Lost." Zhao Si suggests that when she wrote this poem she was thinking of a Scottish ballad (untraceable) that may have contained lines such as "My baby, laugh loud on my knees, when you grow up, you'll have much grief…"

"Epitaph." The line "like lying on the waveless bottom full fathom five" is a reference to Ariel's song overheard by Ferdinand as he recovered from the shipwreck in Shakespeare's *The Tempest*: "full fathom five thy father lies." At the root of the poem is a Chinese idiom that the poet loves – "Hui Tou Tu Lian" – which translates literally as 'ash," "head," and "soil face."

"That Line." EGGs is the abbreviation of "Evaporating Gaseous Globules." The "beginning" and "end" in the line "hence come the names beginning and end." are "qi dian" and "zhong dian" which both has "point" ("dian") in Chinese.

BIOGRAPHIES

THE AUTHOR

Zhao Si (b. 1972) is a Chinese poet, essayist, translator, poetics scholar, editor, and the author or translator of 15 books, including: *White Crow* (poems, 2005); *Gold-in-Sand Picker* (prose poems, 2005); *Disappearing, Recalling: 2009–2014 New Selected Poems* (2016), which won the "2014 Major Support Project" from the China Writers Association; *Matchstick Man* (U.S. publication, 2017), *Zmiznutia a návraty* (2018 – the first book of contemporary Chinese poetry published in Slovakia); translator of two poetry books by Tomaž Šalamun: *Light-Blue-Pillow Tower* (2014) and *The Enormous Boiling Mouths of the Sun* (2016); co-translator of *Edmond Jabès: Complete Poems* (2019); *Selected Poems of Tim Lilburn* (2020, realized by way of a translation grant from the Canada Council for the Arts); Czechia's Vladimír Holan, *A Night with Hamlet* (2022, published with the long essay *Orphic Poets*); *Crow* (2023) and *Season Songs* (2023) by Ted Hughes; and selected works by Hart Crane (U.S.), Yannis Ritsos (Greece), Harold Bloom (U.S.), among others. Her poetry has also been translated into 16 languages.

Zhao Si works for *Poetry Periodical,* which is the premier poetry magazine in China. She was awarded the Polish Marii Konopnickiej Poetry Prize in 2012, was an Orion Visiting Artist at the University of Victoria, Canada, in 2017, and won the Polish Jerzego Sulimy-Kaminskiego Literature Medal in 2020. She is currently the Vice-President of the European Medal of Poetry and Art – HOMER – and established, as chief editor, the "Homer Medal Laureates Series" in 2020. She lives in Beijing.

THE TRANSLATORS

Bruce Meyer (b. 1957) is author or editor of 73 books of poetry, short fiction, non-fiction, literary journalism, memoir, portrait photographs, textbooks, and reference books. He received his B.A. and M.A. from the University of Toronto, and his Ph.D. from McMaster University before being the recipient of a Social Sciences and Humanities Research Council of Canada Post-Doctoral Fellowship for his work on World War One Canadian Literature. For Exile Editions, with Barry Callaghan, he co-edited *We Wasn't Pals: Canadian Poetry and Prose of the First World War* (2000 & 2014, Afterword by Margaret Atwood) and was editor of *Cli-Fi: Canadian Tales of Climate Change* (2017) and *That Dammed Beaver: Canadian Laffs, Gaffes, and Humour* (2018). His broadcasts on the *Great Books, Great Poetry,* and *A Novel Idea* for CBC Radio with Michael Enright remain the network's bestselling spoken-word cd series, and his books, *The Golden Thread: A Reader's Journey Through the Great Books* and *Portraits of Canadian Writers* were national best-sellers. He is twice winner of the Gwendolyn MacEwen Prize for Poetry, the E.J. Pratt Gold Medal and Prize for Poetry, and has also won the the Woolf Poetry Prize in Switzerland, the Ruth Cable Memorial Prize, and the IP Silver Medal for Best Book of Poems in North America in 2014 for *The Seasons*. His most recent books are *A Feast of Brief Hopes* (short stories) and *The First Taste: New and Selected Poems*. He was the inaugural Poet Laureate of the City of Barrie, and lives in Barrie where he teaches at Georgian College.

Xuan Yuan (b.1977) earned her Master's Degree in Linguistics and Translation and Interpreting at Guangxi University in Nanning, and has been teaching at the university since. She was a visiting scholar at Morehead State University in the U.S. in 2012. She is also a literary translator, including work by Tomas Lieske, Mischa Andriessen, Maria Barnas, Christopher Merrill, and Anne Waldman (all of which have been published in China's prestigious *Contemporary International Poetry* periodical) and the books *Selected Poems of Patrick Lane* (2021) and *Anthology of Contemporary Dutch Poets* (2022).

Tim Lilburn (b. 1950) has published 12 books of poetry, including *To the River* (1999), *Kill-site* (2003), *Orphic Politics* (2008), *Assiniboia* (2012), *The Names* (2016) and *Harmonia Mundi* (2022). His work has received a Governor General's Award (*Kill-site*), the Saskatchewan Book of the Year Award, the Canadian Authors Association Award, and the Homer Prize among his many accolades. A selection of his poetry is collected in *Desire Never Leaves: The Poetry of Tim Lilburn (2007)*, edited by Alison Calder.

He has produced three books of essays on poetics, eros and politics, and especially environmentalism: *Living in the World as if It Were Home* (1999); *Going Home* (2008); *The Larger Conversation: Contemplation and Place* (2017); a fourth essay collection, *Numinous Seditions: Interiority and Climate Change,* will be released in the autumn of 2023. He has also edited and contributed to two influential essay anthologies on poetics, *Poetry and Knowing* and *Thinking and Singing: Poetry and the Practice of Philosophy.*

Lilburn was a professor, in the Department of Writing, at the University of Victoria, taught philosophy and religious studies at the

University of Saskatchewan and Middlebury College in the U.S. His work has been widely translated and anthologized.

THE AFTERWORD

Xia Kejun (b. 1969) is a Chinese philosopher, art critic, and curator. He received a PhD in philosophy from Wuhan University, and has held fellowships for post-doctoral studies at Universität Freiburg and Université de Strasbourg (following Jean-Luc Nancy). He is a professor at the School of Liberal Arts in Renmin University of China, Beijing.

He has published 20 books (and voluminous articles) including *The Poetry of Posture* (2011); *Infra-Mince: Duchamp and Zhuangzi* (2011); *The Pleasure of Graphic Writing* (2012); *The Body* (2013); *An Awaiting and Unusable People: Zhuangzi and the Second Turning of Heidegger* (2017); *Unthought of Empty in Chinese Philosophy and Aesthetics* (2019); *Useless Literature: Kafka and China* (2020); *Useless Theology: Benjamin, Herdegger and Derrida* (2022); and *Shadows and Veils* (2022).

Xia is an influential critic and curator of contemporary art centred on the topics like Infra-mince Art, Infra-image, and Enchorial-topia, and has curated a series of related exhibitions in China and Europe.